One Word From God Can Change Your Prayer Life

D0040415

Harrison House
Tulsa, Oklahoma

09 08 07 06 05 04 03 02 01 00   10 9 8 7 6 5 4 3 2 1

One Word From God Can Change Your Prayer Life
ISBN 1-57794-198-5   30-0712
Copyright © 2000 by Kenneth Copeland Ministries
Fort Worth, Texas 76192-0001

Published by Harrison House, Inc.
P.O. Box 35035
Tulsa, Oklahoma 74153

Contents

Introduction

One Word From God Can Change Your Life FOREVER!

When the revelation of this statement exploded on the inside of me, it changed the way I think...about everything! I had been praying for several days about a situation that seemed at the time to be overwhelming. I had been confessing the Word of God over it, but that Word had begun to come out of my head and not my heart. I was pushing in my flesh for the circumstance to change. As I made my confession one more time, the Spirit of God seemed to say to me, *Why don't you be quiet?!*

I said, "But, Lord, I'm confessing the Word!"

He answered inside me, *I know it. I heard you. Now just be still and be quiet a little while, and let the Word of God settle down in your spirit. Quit trying to make this thing happen. You're not God. You're not going to be the one to make it happen anyway!*

So I stopped. I stopped that situation in my mind and began to get quiet before the Lord…and this phrase came up in my spirit… **"One word from God can change anything."**

So I started saying that. I said it off and on all day. It came easily because it came from God—not from my own thinking.

Every time I was tempted to worry or think of ideas concerning my circumstances, I'd think, *Yes, just one word from God…*

I noticed when I'd say that, **the peace of God** would come on me. It was so calming. As a result, a habit developed in me. People would bring me issues. They'd say, "Well, what about…" And I'd either say aloud or think to myself, **"Yeah, that may be so, but one word from God will change anything."**

It began to be the answer for everything. If I was watching television and the news-caster was telling about a disaster, and the people being interviewed were saying things to the effect of "Oh, what are we going to do? It's all been blown away, burned up or shook up...," I'd say, **"Yeah, but one word from God can change anything."**

It really developed into a strength for me, and it can for you, too. That's why we've put together the *One Word From God* Book Series...there could be just one word in these inspiring articles that can change your prayer life forever.

You've been searching, seeking help... and God has the answer. He has the one word that can turn your circumstance around and put you on dry ground. He has the one word that gives you all the peace that's in Him. He is your Intercessor. He wants to give you the desires of your heart as you delight yourself in Him. He wants you perfect and entire, wanting nothing (James 1:4).

God loves you. And He has a word for you. One word that can change your life FOREVER!

Kenneth Copeland

The Time to Pray

Chapter 1

"Pray without ceasing."
— 1 THESSALONIANS 5:17

*Gloria
Copeland*

If you have your ear turned toward God these days, I suspect you've heard Him say something to you about prayer. He's been calling you to spend more time in it, to make it a higher priority in your life.

How do I know? Because He's been telling me the same thing. In fact, the more people I talk to about it, the more convinced I am that God is calling all His people to prayer.

The reason is simple. These are the last of the last days. God is ready to move through us in magnificent and supernatural ways. But He can't do that if we're not walking in the spirit. He can't work through people who are so busy with the affairs of the flesh that they can't hear His voice.

He needs people who will pray—not just when they happen to think about it, but every day. He needs people who will build their whole lives around prayer and make it their number one priority.

Have you ever noticed how Jesus operated when He was on the earth? He placed great importance on prayer. His prayer life was absolutely amazing. The night before He chose the 12 disciples, He was in prayer all night long!

Well, Jesus didn't do things one way and tell us to do something else. He expects us to follow His example.

First Thessalonians 5:17 tells us to *"pray without ceasing."* Ephesians 6:18 tells us to pray *"always with all prayer and supplication in the Spirit."* All through the New Testament we're told to pray! And now it's time for us to do our job. I don't mean just one or two of us—I mean the whole army of God.

Your natural human reaction to that call for prayer may be to say, "Hey, I hardly have time enough to handle all the crises in my life as it is now. I can't afford to spend any more time in prayer!" But, the truth is, you can't afford not to. You need to tap into what time spent with the Father can do for you.

That's what I did. Some time ago, God spoke to me that if I'd give Him a tithe of my time—just an hour or two a day in the Word and prayer—all would be well with me. And not only with me, but that I'd be a blessing to the people around me.

He's made that same promise to you. It's right there for you to read in Romans 8:28. There the Holy Spirit says: *"And we know that all things work together for good to them that love God, to them who are the called according to his purpose."*

Most people take that verse out of context and say the Bible promises that all things (including demonic things like sickness, death and poverty) work together for good, period. But that's not true. If you'll back up and read the surrounding scriptures, you'll find that promise follows a discussion about praying aided by the Holy Spirit—where the Holy Spirit makes intercession for us according to the will of God. Remember Romans 8:26 says He helps us to pray. This is not something the Holy Spirit does apart from us. *The Amplified Bible* says He comes to our aid and bears us up in our weakness when we don't know how to pray as we ought. By His help, we pray in the spirit the perfect will of God!

It's when we begin to make prayer our priority—to lay aside the natural things and take up the things of God and walk in the power of the Spirit—that the glory of God will be reflected in us.

If we want to have the power of God in our lives, we have to get rid of this tunnel vision we've had. We have to quit spending all our time thinking about our little surroundings, our little life, and what we're doing day to day. We have to start giving ourselves to things that will make an eternal difference. We have to start giving ourselves to prayer.

You know God hasn't put us here on the earth just so we could make it through life in relative comfort and then go on to heaven. He's put us here so we can dominate the world of the natural while we're here and do His works just as His Son, Jesus, did. Jesus said we would do even greater works than He did (John 14:12).

But we're not going to be empowered to do those things by sitting around watching television. We're going to be empowered to do them when we start making Jesus' priorities our priorities. When we start wanting what He wants more than anything else.

God has glorious plans for us in the spirit realm. But if we don't spend time in that realm, praying and listening to God, we're not going to get in on those plans.

I heard a story some time ago about some Eastern European believers that illustrates what I'm talking about. It took place a few years ago when the underground church in Eastern Europe had to meet out in the woods and in secret places to keep from being raided by the KGB.

During that time, there was this one group of believers who had a spy among them. As a result, no matter where they met, the police always showed up. So, do you know what they did? They stopped announcing the location of the next meeting. They simply said, "We'll meet wherever the Holy Spirit tells us to. So whoever wants to be there will have to listen to the Spirit to find out where to go." The next time they met, every person showed up except one.

All of us have the ability to listen to our spirit like that. In America, we've not operated in that realm very much. But we're going to. How are we going to? By praying in the spirit and listening to God! The more we do that, the more accurately we'll hear.

Think of your spirit like a kind of inner radio. If you don't tune it to exactly the right frequency, all you get is static and meaningless noise. But if you tune in to the station exactly, everything comes in loud and clear.

God is wanting us to fine-tune ourselves in the realm of the spirit. He's wanting us to tune our spirit so we can pick Him up clearly and definitely. He wants us to be able to hear His voice so we can obey it.

Most, however, haven't been willing to take the time to do that. We've come to the point where if we knew God wanted us to do something, we'd do it. But we won't get quiet before Him long enough to hear Him say what He wants us to do.

That's why He's telling us to put prayer first, to make communication with Him top priority, to shut out the world and spend time in prayer and in the Word. When we do that, He can begin to fine-tune our spirit to hear His voice. His voice is indistinct to us because we spend so much of our time caught up in natural things.

As we begin to come into this place of hearing, we'll be in one accord because we'll all know what the mind of the Spirit is. We'll have our minds and hearts in tune with what God's doing—and then when we come together, there will be an explosion of God's power that will turn the world upside down!

This calling to live in the spirit and in power is drawing us forward. In my spirit, I can see it like a carrot dangling in front of a horse. It is so close to us. All we have to do to reach it is to take a few more steps, to learn to listen to the Spirit of God, and make the adjustments He tells us to make.

I tell you, it's exciting. I've seen enough of the kind of life that's available in God to know that there's not anything in the world more valuable. But if you're going to lay hold of it, you're going to have to get quiet and pray. You're going to have to get unbusy with the affairs of life. You're going to have to set aside all the clamor of the world and get with God.

"Oh, Gloria," you say, "you just don't know how hectic my life is. I just can't do that!"

Yes, you can. It's just a matter of rearranging your priorities.

Think of it this way. If you walked through your kitchen tomorrow morning on your way to work and Jesus was sitting at your kitchen table, what would you do? Would you say, "Jesus! I'm so glad to see You! I wish I had time to visit. If I'd gotten up earlier, I could spend some time with You. But I watched television so late last night and I've been so busy lately—so much work at the office and everything. How about I try to catch You later?"

Ridiculous, isn't it? What would you really do if Jesus were physically sitting at your kitchen table in the morning?

You'd fall on your face before Him. You'd hang on to every moment and say, "I'm not going to work today, Jesus. There are so many things we need to talk about. I can't pass up an opportunity like this."

It wouldn't matter that you were tired. It wouldn't matter how busy things were at the office. You'd get before Him and begin to worship and enjoy times of refreshing from the presence of the Lord until your body wasn't tired any longer.

Do you understand that Jesus actually is closer than your breakfast table? His Spirit is in you—waiting to fellowship with you. When you're tempted to sleep late tomorrow, think about that.

Think about the sweet Spirit of God saying, *I want to help you this morning. I'm here to strengthen you. You know that problem you've been having? I want to apply spiritual power to it so it will disappear from your life.*

Think about the fact that God is waiting on you. That He has some things He wants to show you. Things you've been beating your head against the wall trying to figure out. He's just waiting to counsel you, to show you the answer.

I'll tell you this: God is not going to make you pray. Jesus is not going to make you pray. The Holy Spirit is not going to make you pray. But they are all three calling you to it. They're preparing to go into action the moment you begin.

The eternal, all-powerful Creator of heaven and earth, the Almighty God, is ready right now to meet with you in prayer. He's made your prayers His priority. The question is, have you?

Principles of Effective Prayer

"Be careful for nothing; but in every thing by prayer and supplication with thanksgiving let your requests be made known unto God."

— PHILIPPIANS 4:6

Kenneth Copeland

Have you ever had so many needs that you felt like a prophet would have to pray all night to get them taken care of?

I have!

Shortly after becoming a Christian, I requested prayer for my financial needs. I expected the preacher to make such inspired intercession that everyone would fall on their knees. I imagined him weeping over my problems as Jesus wept over Lazarus' death. But to my amazement, he merely laid his hand on my chest, bowed his head and said, "Lord, bless him. Meet his every need, in the Name of Jesus." Then he turned and walked away!

What a disappointment! My problems were BIG! I figured it would take a BIG prayer to cover them. But you see, I was operating in unbelief, and this man of God was operating in faith. He was concentrating on the answer—Jesus—and not on my problems.

Since then, I've learned a lot about prayer. I've stepped beyond shooting scattershot prayers, just hoping for something to happen, and I've learned to follow the guidelines to prayer that are given in the Word of God. You see, God never meant for us to stumble around in the dark when we pray. Philippians 4:6 says, *"Be careful for nothing; but in every thing by prayer and supplication with thanksgiving let your requests be made known unto God."* God intends to answer our requests. He wants us to get results when we pray. But first, we have to put away our childish ideas about prayer and replace them with God's power-packed principles.

For example, one thing we need to learn is that it is not the length of our prayers that gets results.

According to 1 John 3:22-23: *"Whatsoever we ask, we receive of him, because we keep his commandments, and do those things that are pleasing in his sight. And this is his commandment, That we should believe on the name of his Son Jesus Christ, and love one another, as he gave us commandment."*

Praying all night is not what gets the ear of God; it is believing on and praying in the Name of Jesus. Praying all night is quite an accomplishment, but praying in the Name of Jesus is basing your prayer on His accomplishments, not on yours.

Of course, if you haven't been living a life that is pleasing to God, your prayers will be hindered. Disobedience robs you of your confidence in Him, but even then Jesus is still the answer. He is your Advocate with the Father. Don't run from God when you sin; run to Him! Act on 1 John 1:9. Confess your sin and receive your forgiveness. Don't let sin and condemnation keep God from moving in your life, your heart and your circumstances. Jesus is faithful and just to forgive you when you repent. He wants to answer your prayers.

Another key to answered prayer is praying according to the will of God. The problem is that many believers are in the dark about God's will. Religion has told us, "You never know what God's going to do." But that's not true! He's told us in His Word exactly what He will do.

The written Word brings the will of God out of the realm of obscurity. When we pray in line with the Word, we pray according to the will of God. When we let the Word of God engineer our prayer, *"this is the confidence that we have in him, that, if we ask any thing according to his will, he heareth us: And if we know that he hear us, whatsoever we ask, we know that we have the petitions that we desired of him"* (1 John 5:14-15).

Prayer based on the Word begins with the answer and doesn't concentrate on the problem. Let's take healing as an example. First Peter 2:24 says that by the stripes that Jesus bore, we were healed. Just as in the forgiveness of your sins, your healing was provided for through the Cross. If the Word says you were healed, then God's will is for you to be well. Let the Word of God settle the issue once and for all. Throw out all the arguments, and believe the Word.

Mark 11:24 says, *"What things soever ye desire, when ye pray, believe that ye receive them, and ye shall have them."* Notice that it says for you to believe when you pray. Make the decision that God's Word is absolutely true. If God said that you were healed, then believe that you were healed when you prayed, not when you began to feel better.

When you base your prayer on the fact that the answer is already yours, then the only thing left is to begin the application of your faith. Faith is your response to what God has already provided.

Faith is released in two ways: by saying it and by acting on it. If 1 Peter 2:24 says you were healed, then don't say, "I'm sick." Say, "I believe that by the stripes Jesus bore for me, I am healed." And then act like it. Real Bible believing demands action.

If someone came running in your front door and said, "The house is on fire!" and you believed it, you would immediately get out. You wouldn't wait until you saw smoke!

23

Faith in God's Word works the same way. Don't wait until you feel healed to believe it. Believe it before anything you can see ever happens, or it will never happen. Faith makes prayer work; prayer doesn't make faith work.

If your needs have been piling up, don't panic. Pray! Your spiritual, mental, physical, financial and social needs can be met by the power of Almighty God. Just follow God's principles of prayer and make your requests known unto Him; then start to praise, knowing the results are on the way!

Trade in Your Old Prayers

"Delight thyself also in the Lord; and he shall give thee the desires of thine heart."
— PSALM 37:4

John Avanzini

If your prayers are going unanswered lately, it may be time to trade in your old prayers for some more accurate ones. God answers only those prayers that are in agreement with His will (1 John 5:14). So check your prayers to be sure what you're praying lines up with His will.

There are three steps to finding out what God wants you to pray.

First, study the Word. God's Word is His will, and you'll never know what His will is without knowing His Word intimately (2 Timothy 2:15).

Second, renew your mind. The study of God's Word will transform you so you can know what is the good, acceptable and perfect will of God (Romans 12:2).

Third, be soft and pliable to God's will for your life. Be ready to replace your desires with God's desires. That may sound difficult, but it's actually easy if you follow God's directions.

Psalm 37:4 says, *"Delight thyself also in the Lord; and he shall give thee the desires of thine heart."* The Hebrew word translated *delight* means "be soft and pliable." So we could say, "Be soft and pliable in the hands of God, and He will give you the desires of your heart."

But if that were all God meant, we would soon be in big trouble. Most of our own desires are not God's desires for us. God isn't saying He'll give us whatever we desire if we are merely soft and pliable. He's saying He will cause our desires to be taken out of our hearts and replaced with His own desires. As we become soft and pliable in His hands, we will exchange our desires for the things He desires.

When what we desire is what God desires for us, we can pray accurately. Let God tell you what to pray, and your prayers will always be answered!

Into His Courts With Praise

"I will praise thee, O Lord, with my whole heart; I will show forth all thy marvellous works. I will be glad and rejoice in thee."
— PSALM 9:1-2

Kenneth Copeland

For verily I say unto you, That whosoever shall say unto this mountain, Be thou removed, and be thou cast into the sea; and shall not doubt in his heart, but shall believe that those things which he saith shall come to pass; he shall have whatsoever he saith. Therefore I say unto you, What things soever ye desire, when ye pray, believe that ye receive them, and ye shall have them (Mark 11:23-24).

This very familiar scripture has to do with praying in faith, or praying to get results. The most important thing for you to remember about praying accurately is to go to the Word of God, find out what the Word says about the problem and then pray according to that Word.

First John 5:14-15 says when we ask anything according to His will, we know He hears us and we know we have the petitions we desired of Him. When you pray according to God's Word, which is His will, then you know that your prayer is answered.

Jesus said, *"Whatsoever ye shall ask the Father in my name, he will give it you"* (John 16:23). When you use the Name of Jesus in prayer, you get the ear of God.

Peter wrote that the eyes of God are over the righteous and His ears are open to their prayers. You don't have to pray until you get God's attention. He is listening for your prayer. You have His attention all the time.

When you pray according to Mark 11:23-24, you believe you receive when you pray. This opens the door for thanksgiving and praise. Philippians 4:6 says, *"Be careful for nothing; but in every thing by prayer and supplication with thanksgiving let your*

requests be made known unto God."
Thanksgiving and praise are an integral part
of prayer. When you believe you receive,
then you begin to praise God for the answer.
You thank God that it is done for you.

Thanksgiving and praise involve more
than just speaking lovely words to God.
There is power in the praise of God. Praise
was ordained by God for a definite reason.
It serves a purpose.

Psalms 8 and 9 point out some things
about praise that every believer should know.
Psalm 8:1-2 says, *"O Lord our Lord, how
excellent is thy name in all the earth! who
hast set thy glory above the heavens. Out of
the mouth of babes and sucklings hast thou
ordained strength because of thine enemies,
that thou mightest still the enemy and the
avenger."* Jesus quoted that passage in
Matthew 21:16: *"Out of the mouth of
babes and sucklings thou hast perfected
praise."* He equates praise with strength.

From these scriptures, we see that God
brought praise into existence. He ordained
it. Why? *"Because of thine enemies, that thou
mightest still the enemy and the avenger."*

Praise stops Satan right in his tracks. It is a weapon we are to use in calling a halt to Satan's maneuvers. Psalm 9 says: *"I will praise thee, O Lord, with my whole heart; I will show forth all thy marvellous works. I will be glad and rejoice in thee: I will sing praise to thy name, O thou most High. When mine enemies are turned back, they shall fall and perish at thy presence. For thou hast maintained my right and my cause; thou satest in the throne judging right"* (verses 1-4).

When your enemies are turned back...not *if.* There is no question about it. Remember: We wrestle not against flesh and blood, but against Satan's forces. When you praise God, your enemies have to turn back. They will fall and perish at your presence. You can see why praise is so important in the life of a believer. It is a vital weapon in your warfare against Satan and his forces.

Usher in His Presence

One thing you must realize is that praise is not governed by emotions. God is worthy of your praise whether you feel like praising Him or not. Hebrews 13:15 says, *"Let us offer the sacrifice of praise to God continually, that is, the fruit of our lips giving thanks to his name."* Under the Old Covenant, when the people had problems, they went to the priest and he would offer a sacrifice to God. That would bring God on the scene.

Today, under the New Covenant, we are to do the same. We are priests under God (Revelation 5:10). As we offer up the sacrifices of praise before our Most High Priest, Jesus, our communication with God is great. Psalm 22:3 says God inhabits the praises of His people. Praise brings God on the scene personally. At times of high praise, the shekinah glory of God will fill the whole place with His sweet presence.

When Solomon finished building the house of the Lord, the trumpeters and singers lifted their voices as one and, with trumpets, cymbals and instruments of music, they praised the Lord saying, *"For he is good; for his mercy endureth for ever."* The glory of God filled the house so that the priests could not even minister because of the cloud

31

(2 Chronicles 5:13-14). God Himself inhabited the praises of His people.

Jehoshaphat appointed singers unto the Lord to go before the army and say, *"Praise the Lord; for his mercy endureth for ever."*

When the Israelites began to sing and praise, the Lord set ambushments against their enemies, and their enemies destroyed themselves (2 Chronicles 20:21-23).

The weapon of praise! Singers going before an army? It happened just that way. Israel didn't have to unsheathe a weapon of war. They only had to sing *"Praise the Lord; for his mercy endureth for ever."*

David was a man after God's own heart. He knew how to praise his God. Until you have the Word dwelling in you richly so that you can speak psalms and praises out of your own spirit, use the praises of David to magnify God. Speak them or sing them out loud to the Father.

> **In God I will praise his word, in God I have put my trust; I will not fear what flesh can do unto me. Every day they wrest my words: all**

their thoughts are against me for evil. They gather themselves together, they hide themselves, they mark my steps, when they wait for my soul... I cry unto thee, then shall mine enemies turn back: this I know; for God is for me. In God will I praise his word: in the Lord will I praise his word. In God have I put my trust: I will not be afraid what man can do unto me (Psalm 56:4-6, 9-11).

The Bible says God inhabits the praises of His people (Psalm 22:3). The enemy is turned back, falls and perishes at the presence of our God.

Praise not only honors God and empowers our faith, but it is also a powerful weapon in the realm of the spirit. Remember: Praise will cause Satan and his forces to turn back, fall and perish at your presence.

Keep the Door Open

Abraham *"grew strong and was empowered by faith as he gave praise and glory to God"* (Romans 4:20, AMP). As you praise

God and speak of His marvelous works, your faith rises on the inside of you to receive the blessings of God.

Honor God with the words of your mouth. Allow your words to agree with God's words where He is concerned. Look in His Word for *good things* to proclaim about Him. Publish the Lord's mercy and compassion to those around you. Tell others of the great things He has done in your life.

Notice that David said, *"I will praise... I will show forth all thy marvellous works... I will be glad and rejoice...I will sing praise"* (Psalm 9:1-2). It is a matter of your will. You do not just praise God because you feel like it. You praise God because you *will* to praise Him. Say with David, *"I will praise thee, O Lord, with my whole heart."* Then watch the Word go to work on your behalf!

One incident during Jesus' earthly ministry clearly shows the importance that praise can have. Luke 17:12-19 describes the cleansing of 10 lepers. All 10 of them were cleansed, but only one turned back to Jesus and glorified God. To that one man,

Jesus said, *"Arise, go thy way: thy faith hath made thee whole."* The others were *cleansed.* He was *made whole.*

As I was meditating on these scriptures, the Lord showed me a vision. I saw the man come running up to Jesus. He was cleansed—all the disease was gone from his body—but the bottom of his ear was missing. The disease had eaten it away. As he shouted and praised God, the ear was restored. He was *made whole.* Praise made the difference.

If you do not know very much about praising God, then I encourage you to spend time meditating in the Word concerning praise. It will revolutionize your life! I guarantee it! David said, *"I will show forth all [Your] marvellous works."* If you don't know how to praise God, just find some of the things God has already done throughout the Bible and begin to praise Him for doing them. When I first began doing these things, I would open my Bible and praise God by reading the Psalms out loud. From there I let the Holy Spirit lead me into praising God for things He had done in my life and to saying things that would bless God.

One important thing I have learned is to praise God in the spirit. The real strength comes when we praise the Lord in the spirit, in other tongues. First Corinthians 14:4 says we are edified, or charged up, when we speak in tongues. First Corinthians 14:17 says giving thanks in tongues is giving thanks well. Praising God in this way enables us to praise Him beyond our own intellects. We allow the Holy Spirit to lead us into unlimited praise and thanksgiving. This is surely perfected praise (Matthew 21:16).

Let's say you are faced with a problem. You know what the Word says about it, so you go directly to prayer. You put your faith into action against the mountain—whatever it may be. You pray and believe God for the answer. By believing God in that situation and acting on the Word, you are applying faith power to the mountain. It begins to move. Then Satan gets involved. The only way he can stop you is by injecting unbelief so that you will stop applying pressure to the mountain. He can't stop the mountain from being moved, but he can try to stop you from applying the pressure of your faith to it. The mountain will never move until you apply the faith force necessary to move it. This is where praise comes in.

While you are standing in faith—while you are applying the Word of God to the situation—it is important to keep the praise of God on your lips. Continue to praise God for the answer. Praise Him that the mountain is moved. Don't be moved by the circumstances. Just keep your eyes on God's Word. The Word of God and prayer open the doors for God's power to work. Praise keeps them open. Praise will bring manifestations of the Holy Spirit and His great power.

Activate the power of God in every area of your life by speaking the Word in faith and praising God that His marvelous works have been performed on your behalf.

The Power of Praying in Tongues

"But you, beloved, build your-selves up [founded] on your most holy faith—make progress, rise like an edifice higher and higher—praying in the Holy Spirit."
— JUDE 20, AMP

Gloria Copeland

You have a weakness. It doesn't matter who you are...or how often you work out at the local gym. If you're a born-again child of God living on planet Earth, you have a weakness. It's a weakness that can knock your legs out from under you just when you think you're standing strong. It can cause you to act like a sinner on the outside when on the inside you're a saint.

What is that weakness? Your flesh.

That's right. That flesh-and-blood body you live in hasn't been reborn as your spirit has. If it controls your life, it will take you from one failure to another. And believe me, if you don't do something to stop it, it will take control.

What you have to do is build up your spirit—strengthen it to the point where it can actually dominate, or rule over, your flesh. If that sounds hard, don't worry. It's not. In fact, God has made it so easy that anyone can do it. Jude 20 will show you how. It says: *"But you, beloved, build yourselves up [founded] on your most holy faith—make progress, rise like an edifice higher and higher—praying in the Holy Spirit"* (AMP).

Most believers don't realize it, but praying in the spirit, or praying in other tongues, is a spiritual exercise that strengthens your inner man. Just as barbells build up your arms, praying in tongues will build up your spirit. If you'll do it faithfully, it will help bring you to the point where your spirit will be able to keep that fleshly body of yours in line.

"Well, Gloria," you may ask, "why can't I just do that by praying in English?"

Because the Bible says your "weakness" gets in the way. Many times your natural mind doesn't have the first idea how to pray as it needs to. It may not know how to pray prayers that will strengthen you against temptations that are about to come your way. Your mind is not informed as your spirit is. Your spirit is in contact with God. That's why, as Romans 8:26-28 says:

> The (Holy) Spirit comes to our aid and bears us up in our weakness; for we do not know what prayer to offer nor how to offer it worthily as we ought, but the Spirit Himself goes to meet our supplication and pleads in our behalf with unspeakable yearnings and groanings too deep for utterance. And He who searches the hearts of men knows what is in the mind of the (Holy) Spirit...because the Spirit intercedes and pleads [before God] in behalf of the saints according to and in harmony with God's will (AMP).

Praying in the spirit enables you to pray the perfect will of God for your life. It allows you to step out of the realm of the flesh and into the realm of the spirit so that no matter how weak or ignorant you may be in the natural, you can pray exactly as you need to.

Is it any wonder that speaking in tongues has undergone such persecution—to the point where people were even killed for it in our own country? The devil hates it! He knows it's the only way believers can pray beyond what they know.

He understands (even if we don't) that even baby Christians, newly reborn, can pray in tongues, get the mind of the Spirit, and start growing fast. That's the way the church at Jerusalem grew in the early days, you know. That's all they had. They couldn't turn to the book of Ephesians or the book of Colossians. They just had to use the ability and understanding the Holy Spirit had given them. And when they did, they turned the whole world upside down.

Let me tell you something. This will turn your world upside down too. Or, it might be more accurate to say, it will turn it right side up. It will pump you up and enable you to walk in the power of the Spirit instead of the weakness of the flesh.

But be warned, it won't work for you unless you put it to work. The Holy Spirit is a gentleman. He's not going to come storming in and make you pray in the spirit. He's going to wait on you to decide to do it. He's going to wait for you to put your will in gear.

What happens if you don't? You won't be prepared when trouble comes.

In Luke 21:36, Jesus says, *"Watch ye therefore, and pray always, that ye may be accounted worthy* [or, as *The Amplified Bible* says, *'that you may have the full strength and ability'*] *to escape all these things that shall come to pass."*

If you want to have the strength and ability to come through troubled times in triumph, you'd better spend some time in prayer.

That's what Jesus urged Peter and the other disciples to do in the Garden of Gethsemane. He knew they were about to face one of the toughest times of their lives. He said, *"Watch ye and pray, lest ye enter into temptation. The spirit truly is ready, but the flesh is weak"* (Mark 14:38).

But the Scripture tells us they didn't obey Him. They slept instead. And, in Peter's life in particular, we can see the result. When temptation came, he entered into it and denied the Lord.

You might as well face it. Temptation is going to come to you as long as you live in a flesh body. So you'd better be prepared. You'd better have spent some time praying in the spirit when it comes.

If you've spent much time with the Lord at all, these instructions probably don't come as much of a surprise to you. In fact, I strongly suspect that God has already been speaking to you about spending more time praying in the spirit.

I remember when He first began to speak to me about the importance of it. I'd been asking Him to show me how to quit living my life so much on the natural, circumstantial level and start walking in the spirit. *Pray an hour or two a day in the spirit* was the first instruction He gave me.

I'd been committed to the Word for years at that time. I regularly spent much time reading and meditating on it—and that alone had already revolutionized my life. But I knew there was still something lacking.

What God showed me was that it was time to add to the Word by praying more in the spirit. It's really so simple, I'm surprised I didn't see it before. First Corinthians 14:14 says, *"If I pray in an unknown tongue, my spirit prayeth."* So when I began to pray more in tongues, I began to give my spirit more outflow. I gave vent to it.

Giving vent to your spirit is the way you walk in the spirit, just as giving vent to your flesh is the way you walk in the flesh. The more I released my spirit through tongues, the more it began to take charge. And I found it worked just as the Bible says: *"Walk in the spirit, and ye shall not fulfil the lust of the flesh"* (Galatians 5:16). I found it easier to hear and obey my spirit indwelt by the Holy Spirit.

Simple, isn't it? But the devil has tried to hide the simplicity of it from us because he knows if we ever start doing it he'll have no place left. You see, he's limited. He can't touch your reborn spirit. The only thing he has to work on is your flesh. Once you learn what brings the flesh under dominion—once you learn that praying in the spirit applies spirit to flesh and causes the flesh to obey God the way it ought to—the devil won't be able to get a foothold in your life at all!

But listen, the benefits of praying in tongues don't stop there. In fact, that's just the beginning! Listen to what the Apostle Paul wrote about it: *"For he that speaketh in an unknown tongue speaketh not unto men, but unto God: for no man understandeth him; howbeit in the spirit he speaketh mysteries"* (1 Corinthians 14:2).

What are mysteries? Mysteries are things we don't know. We don't just automatically know, for example, what the perfect will of God is for our lives. We don't know exactly what part we've been called to play in the Body of Christ. We don't know exactly what steps to take and what moves to make each day to fulfill the plan God has laid out for our lives.

And nobody in the world can tell us! As 1 Corinthians 2:9-10 says, *"Eye hath not seen, nor ear heard, neither have entered into the heart of man, the things which God hath prepared for them that love him. But God hath revealed them unto us by his Spirit!"*

"But how can all those things be revealed to me if I'm praying in a language I don't understand?"

They can't. That's why the Bible tells us to pray that we might interpret. As you begin to pray in the spirit, ask God to give you an understanding of what He's saying. You might not get the interpretation immediately, but eventually it will begin to bubble up inside you. You'll get an impression. A word. A sentence. Say to the Lord, "The things I know not, teach me, and the things I see not, show me." You'll begin to get revelation on things you've never understood before.

That's what you need: Revelation from God! That's what we all need. You know, we're not nearly as smart as we think we are. God has things that are so far better for us than what we've seen that we can't

47

even figure them out. But if we'll pray in the spirit, we'll get into that area out beyond our knowledge and expectation, *"above all that we ask or think,"* as the Bible puts it (Ephesians 3:20).

I'll tell you this. If we all start praying the will of God by the power of the Spirit, this age is going to come to an end quickly! God will be able to get mysteries into the earth. He'll be able to use our mouths and our authority to call forth His plan in the earth.

And, praise God, every one of us—from the least to the greatest—can participate because it's so simple! Every one of us can pray in tongues every day if we choose. You don't even have to be smart to do it. But without a doubt, if you'll do it, it will one day prove to be the smartest thing you ever did.

What Do You Want?

Chapter 6

"Let patience have her perfect work, that ye may be perfect and entire, wanting nothing."
— JAMES 1:4

Jeanne Caldwell

My child, what do you want of Me?

With this simple question, God revealed to me a powerful principle of prayer: To be effective, your prayers must be specific. In order to answer your prayers, God has to know exactly what you want.

Here are some guidelines which will help you pray correctly, specifically and effectively:

First, go to the Father in the Name of Jesus and make your requests known. Then, believe that you receive when you pray, and if you have anything against any person, forgive him (Mark 11:24-25).

Second, stand on the promises in God's Word that cover your need. Be specific. Make a prayer list and stick to it. Pray for what you specifically need and what you are specifically believing for, one item at a time.

Third, be patient! *"Rest in the Lord, and wait patiently for him"* (Psalm 37:7). As long as your prayer lines up with God's Word, He will answer at the right time—His time. So relax, and *"let patience have her perfect work, that ye may be perfect and entire, wanting nothing"* (James 1:4).

Finally, but most important of all, develop a loving relationship with your Heavenly Father. Get to know Him intimately, and you will have unshakable confidence in Him and in His Word.

Specific prayers receive specific answers. Always remember, *"If we ask any thing according to [God's] will, he heareth us: And if we know that he hear us, whatsoever we ask, we know that we have the petitions that we desired of him"* (1 John 5:14-15).

The Place of Prayer

"And it shall come to pass in the last days, saith God, I will pour out of my Spirit upon all flesh."
— ACTS 2:17

Kenneth Copeland

There is a particular phrase I've heard spoken countless times over the years, and I like it less every time I hear it. No doubt, you've heard it too.

It comes most frequently on the heels of some tragedy. It's said—usually in drawn-out, religious-sounding tones—when circumstances seem to fall short of what God has promised us in His Word.

The phrase is "Well, Brother, you have to remember...God is sovereign."

As spiritual as that phrase might sound, it really bothers me. It's not that I don't believe God is sovereign. Certainly He is. According to Webster's Dictionary, *sovereign* means "above or superior to all others; supreme in power, rank or authority." Without question, God is all those things.

But all too often, when people refer to the sovereignty of God, what they're actually saying is, "You never know what God will do. After all, He's all powerful and totally independent, so He does whatever He wants whenever He wants."

The problem with that view of sovereignty is it releases us of all responsibility. After all, if God is sovereign, He will do what He wants anyway, so we might as well go watch *Gunsmoke* and forget about it, right?

Wrong. After more than 30 years of studying the Word and preaching the gospel, I've come to realize that God does very few things—if any—in this earth without man's cooperation. Even though it belongs to God—it is His creation and He owns it. Psalm 8:6 tells us God has made man *"to have dominion over the works of [God's] hands."*

God Himself put mankind in charge. He doesn't intervene in the affairs of earth whenever He wants. He respects the dominion and authority He has given us. So until man's lease on this planet expires, God restricts His power on the earth, taking action only when He is asked to do so.

Since the people who do the asking (the intercessors) are often very quiet people who do their praying in secret, it may appear at times that God simply acts on His own. But regardless of appearances, the Bible teaches from cover to cover that God's connection with man is a prayer and faith connection. When you see Him act in a mighty way, you can be sure there was someone somewhere praying and interceding to bring Him on the scene.

More Than Spectators

Now more than ever before, it is vital for every Christian to understand that. We are in the last of the last days. We are on the edge of the greatest outpouring of God's glory this earth has ever seen. Amazing, supernatural things are beginning to happen just as the Bible said they would.

Yet many believers are just sitting back, watching these events like spiritual spectators. They seem to think God will sovereignly turn over some great heavenly glory bucket and spill signs and wonders over the earth. But it won't happen that way.

How will it happen? Acts 2:17-19 shows us:

> **And it shall come to pass in the last days, saith God, I will pour out of my Spirit upon all flesh: and your sons and your daughters shall prophesy, and your young men shall see visions, and your old men shall dream dreams: And on my servants and on my handmaidens I will pour out in those days of my Spirit; and they shall prophesy: And I will show wonders in heaven above, and signs in the earth beneath.**

If you'll read the last part of that passage again, taking out the punctuation that was put in by the translators, you'll see a divine connection most people miss. You'll see that God is saying when His servants and handmaidens prophesy, when they speak out His divine will and purpose in intercession and faith, then, in response to their speaking, He will work signs and wonders.

That means if this last outpouring of glory is to come in its fullness, all of God's servants and handmaidens must be in their place. What place?

The place of prayer!

Some people would say, "Well, Brother Copeland, we're talking about end-time events here, and I believe God will simply bring them about on His own. He doesn't need any help from us. After all, those things are too important to entrust to mere men."

That's what I used to think too. But God set me straight some years ago. At the time, I had been studying the authority of man and had seen over and over in His Word how the prayers of God's people precede God's actions on the earth. Yet I still hung on to the idea that God still did His most important works independently of man.

One day as I was praying about it, I said, "Lord, You brought Jesus into the earth sovereignly, didn't You?"

No, I didn't, He answered.

"You mean there were people who interceded for the birth of Jesus?" I asked.

Yes.

Then He told me the names of two of them—Simeon and Anna.

50 Years of Prayer

You can find the scriptural account of these two intercessors in Luke 2. There, the Bible tells us that when Jesus was 8 days old, His parents took Him to the temple to be dedicated to the Lord and circumcised into the Abrahamic covenant.

This ceremony was very sacred to the Jewish people, yet right in the middle of it, a man named Simeon walked in and took the baby Jesus in his arms. Nobody said anything to him. Nobody tried to stop him. So it's obvious he was well-known in the temple as a very spiritual man.

How did Simeon know to go to the temple at that particular time? Was it because somebody came and told him that Jesus was being dedicated? No, the Bible tells us *"he came by the Spirit"* (verse 27). He was led there by God.

What's more, even though Mary herself didn't yet understand Who this child of hers truly was, Simeon did, and he prophesied, saying: *"Lord, now lettest thou thy servant depart in peace, according to thy word: For mine eyes have seen thy salvation, Which thou hast prepared before the face of all people; A light to lighten the Gentiles, and the glory of thy people Israel"* (verses 29-32).

Simeon knew Who Jesus was because he had interceded, asking God to send the Redeemer. He had prayed so fervently and so long that God had promised him *"that he should not see death, before he had seen the Lord's Christ"* (verse 26).

It is amazing enough that Simeon recognized Jesus as the Savior of Israel, but his words reveal he knew even more than that. Read again what Simeon said and you'll see that he knew Jesus was bringing salvation to the Gentiles—a fact the rest of the Church didn't find out until Peter went to Cornelius' house, 10 years after the Day of Pentecost!

Why was Simeon so wise? He was an inter-cessor. Intercessors know things other people don't know. God tells them divine secrets and mysteries. He gives them inside information.

When Simeon finished prophesying over Jesus that day, in walked a little, 84-year-old widow named Anna. Unlike Simeon, this woman didn't have to be led to the temple by the Holy Spirit—she was already there. In fact, the Bible tells us that she *"departed not from the temple, but served God with fast-ings and prayers night and day"* (verse 37).

She hadn't just been there for a week or two, either. She had been residing there ever since her husband died. Since she had only been married seven years and we know from historical records that Jewish women married at about age 16, we can figure she had been praying in the temple for well over 50 years.

That's what I call staying with the program!

Luke 2:38 says that Anna *"coming in that instant gave thanks likewise unto the Lord, and spake of him to all them that looked for redemption in Jerusalem."* No one had to tell her Who Jesus was. She knew the moment she saw Him because, like Simeon, she had been praying for God to send Him for many years.

Just think—even though God is the Almighty, Supreme Creator of this universe, He did not send Jesus into the earth independently. He did it in cooperation with men. He did it in response to the faith-filled words and prayers of His people.

Matthew 18:19 says, *"If two of you shall agree on earth as touching any thing that they shall ask, it shall be done for them of my Father which is in heaven."* Whether Simeon and Anna knew it or not, they were praying in agreement. They had both interceded, asking God to send His Redeemer, and God answered.

Get With the Program!

What does that mean to us today? It means if we want to see the fullness of this final outpouring of glory, we must get with the program as Anna did. We must get on our knees and start praying for it. We must start speaking out God's Word and His will for this last hour in prophecy and intercession so He can do signs and wonders.

You see, there are certain things that will never happen on the earth unless somebody speaks them. If you'll read through the Bible, you'll discover there are certain events that had to be foretold by the prophets before God would bring them to pass.

Now I'm not saying Jesus won't come back if you don't pray. Jesus is coming for His people—and He is coming soon. This world has had all the sin it will stand and it's about to come apart. The whole creation is groaning under the stress of it. God will close out this age just as He said He would in His Word—no matter what you and I do. He'll find a Simeon and an Anna somewhere to get the job done.

But if the whole bunch of us believers will pray, instead of just a few, He'll increase the outpouring of glory that will accompany His return. If we'll cry out to God in one accord as the early Church did in Acts 4, this earth will be shaken by the power of God.

God cannot sit still when He hears the cries of His people!

The problem is, most of God's people are too busy with other things to take the time to intercede and cry out to Him. They don't make prayer a priority. Many are so occupied "working" for God, they think they don't need to pray.

But in the end, we'll find out it was the intercessors who were behind every success in ministry. Someday in heaven when the rewards are being handed out, Brother Big will be sitting on the front row expecting a gold trophy because he started the first church in his county. He'll lean over to the fellow next to him and say, "Yes, amen. I pastored that church for 47 years. I led 2,000 people to the Lord and had 1,000 baptized in the Holy Ghost in 1919. I'll tell you boys all about it as soon as I get my trophy."

But when the Lord starts to give the trophy, instead of calling Brother Big's name, He'll say, "Where's Mother Smith?" Then He'll send an angel down to row 7 million to fly Mother Smith up to the front.

When she gets there, He'll put that trophy in her hands and say, "Mother Smith, I want to give you this in honor of those 25 years you prayed and interceded and lay on your face before Me. Because of your prayers, I called Brother Big to come start the first church in your county. Because of your prayers, thousands of people were saved and filled with the Holy Spirit in that church."

Then He'll turn to the front row and say, "Brother Big, I'm rewarding you by allowing you to carry Mother Smith's trophy for her."

Right Place/Right Time

I can tell you whose trophies I will get to carry when that day comes. One of them will belong to my mother and another will belong to a little woman who used to pray with her all the time. That woman would go into my bedroom and get my pillow off my bed. Then she would carry it with her as she walked the floor and interceded for me, leaving her tears on my pillow. I know full well that's why God wouldn't leave me alone in my bed at night.

I'm saved and preaching the gospel today because of those two women. I don't get any credit for it.

I do have some credit coming for the times I interceded and cried out to God on behalf of someone else. But rewards aren't the reason you pray those kinds of prayers. You pray them because you're a bond-servant of the One Who laid His blood on the line for you. You pray them because of love.

That's the only motivation strong enough, because the job of the intercessor is the toughest job in the kingdom of God. The intercessor carries the spiritual load of every-thing that happens in the Body of Christ, and it's the most thankless ministry that exists.

When we preachers hold meetings where people get born again, most folks think it was our efforts that brought those people to the Lord. But all we did was preach the message God gave us. The anointing necessary to get lost people saved came because of the prayers of the intercessors.

Revival doesn't come from good preaching. Revival comes from prayer. The great sermon Peter preached on the Day of Pentecost didn't come because Peter was such an outstanding fellow. It came because people had been praying in one accord in one place for many days. About 120 of them prayed until the Spirit of God burst on the scene.

Those people "prayed in" that first great outpouring of the Holy Spirit. And when He came, where do you think He manifested Himself first? In the place where they were praying!

God hasn't changed. He is doing the same thing in our day that He did in Acts 2. But this time, He is moving even more powerfully and gloriously than He did then.

Does your heart hunger to experience that end-time outpouring? Do you want to see firsthand the supernatural signs and wonders He will perform in these last days? Then get in the place of prayer! Become an intercessor, yielding to the Spirit of God in prayer and speaking out His will.

If you'll do that, you won't have to be satisfied with second-hand reports of God's glory. You won't have to say, "I wish I had been there."

Like Simeon and Anna, you'll be in the right place at the right time. You'll have inside information because you won't be just a bystander; you'll be helping to bring forth the glorious return of the Lord!

Want a Change? Make a Change

"Solid food is for full-grown men, for those whose senses and mental faculties are trained by practice to discriminate and distinguish...good and...evil."
— HEBREWS 5:14, AMP

Gloria Copeland

If you're new to the things of God, a beginner just learning about the Word of faith, no doubt you're eager to launch into a lifestyle of living contact with God by spending time each day in prayer and the Word. That's how I was too when I first learned what the Word of God could do.

No one had to urge me to put the Word first place. No one had to tell me to turn off the television and put down the newspaper. I totally lost interest in those things because Ken and I had our lives in such bad shape that we were desperate for

God. We were in trouble. We weren't on the bottom of the barrel. We were under the barrel, and it was on top of us.

We knew that the Word of God was the only answer to our desperate situation. So it was easy for us to sell out to it and spend time in the Word and in living contact with God day and night.

You know, desperation sometimes helps. It encourages you to simplify your life. It inspires you to eliminate the unnecessary things and just go for God. But after you've walked with God for a while and things begin to be comfortable, it's easy to lose the desire you once had for the Word.

That's what happened to me. Once Ken and I paid our debts and began enjoying the blessings of God, I began to let too much of my time be taken up by other things. They weren't sinful things; they were just things I enjoyed doing. Almost without realizing it, my appetite for the things of God began to wane. Instead of hungering more for time with Him than for anything else, I enjoyed other activities and interests more. Those activities would have been fine if I had kept them in the right place, but they occupied too much of my time and attention.

I hardly even noticed it had happened until, one day in 1977, I was attending one of Kenneth E. Hagin's meetings and he began to prophesy. (I still keep the final words of that prophecy in my notebook today.) Part of that prophecy said to purpose in your heart that you will not be lazy, that you will not draw back, hold back or sit down, that you will rise up, march forward and become on fire.

When I heard that, it dawned on me that I had let myself slip spiritually. I realized I'd become lazy about the things of God. I was still spending time in the Word, but not as much as before, and I wasn't as full of zeal either. (That will always be the case. You can't be spiritually on fire without spending a sufficient amount of time with God.)

The Lord began to deal with me about it. I prayed and determined in my heart that I would change things. In order to simplify my life, I asked the Lord to show me what activities I should eliminate and what I should take on.

He led me to drop certain things out of my life that were stealing my time with Him. He also told me to do certain things that would help me get back in the habit of spending time with Him as I should. One specific thing He told me to do was to read one of John G. Lake's sermons each day. Brother Lake had such a spirit and revelation of dominion that each time I read one of those sermons, it opened up my heart to the power of God in a fresh way.

He also led me to get up an hour earlier in the morning so I could spend time with Him before I began my day. When I started, it was wintertime. My alarm clock would go off and my flesh would say, *You don't want to get up. It's too dark! It's too cold!* My bed would feel so wonderful and warm that there were a few mornings during the first few weeks that I'd agree with my body and go back to sleep.

I didn't let that stop me though. If I became lazy and went back to sleep, I'd repent. Then I just asked God to help me, and the next morning I'd go at it again! Eventually, my body became trained.

Your body can be trained to follow God just as it can be trained to follow the devil. Hebrews 5:14 says that mature believers have their *"senses and mental faculties...trained by practice to discriminate and distinguish between...good and...evil"* (AMP). If you practice the things of God, your body will eventually begin to cooperate with you.

For me, getting up earlier was a challenge for a while. But eventually my body learned it wouldn't receive that extra hour of sleep anymore, and it stopped complaining. It became accustomed to getting up at that hour. I also believe for supernatural rest when I have a short night. It works!

The decision to make time for God every morning has been one of the most important decisions of my life. It made such a difference in my spiritual growth. I'm not the same person I was then. People are always talking about how timid and restrained I used to be. I really was, too, but I got over it!

Become Addicted to Jesus

By implementing the changes God instructed me to make, I created a lifestyle of living contact with God. I became addicted to spending time with Him. Do you know what the word *addicted* means? It means "to devote, to deliver over, to apply habitually."

You can create good habits in God the same way you can create poor habits. If you'll habitually apply yourself to making contact with Him daily through prayer and the Word, it will become a way of life to you. You won't even have to think about doing it. It will just come naturally to you.

That's what happened to me. I have developed such a habit of making time with God my first priority that I don't have to get up every day and think, *Well, should I read the Word and pray this morning?* I just do it automatically. It's a way of life for me to spend the first part of my day in prayer now. Even when Ken and I are traveling, even when I have to get up at 4 o'clock in the morning to do it—I do it.

You might think that's extreme. You might think I'm the only one around who is that committed to spending time with the Lord every day, but I'm not. I'm one of many.

I have one friend in particular who is very diligent about it. No matter how early she has to get up in the morning, no matter what else her schedule may hold, she puts her time in the Word and in prayer first place in her day. That's because many years ago she found herself dying of liver cancer. The doctors had diagnosed it and told her she only had a few months to live.

Medical science couldn't help her, so she turned to God's medicine. She began to spend time reading and meditating on scriptures about healing each and every day. As a result, she is alive and well today with no trace of cancer in her body.

My friend knows she owes her very life to God's Word, so she is still faithful and diligent to partake of those scriptures and fellowship with God first thing every morning. She and her husband are ministers of the gospel and, like Ken and I, they often begin their day very early. But she says, "Even if I have to get up at 3 a.m., I'll do it."

Certainly such faithfulness requires time and effort. It's not easy. But if believers fully understood the blessings it brings, they too would be willing to do whatever was necessary in order to make their time with God their first priority every day.

There are great rewards for that kind of faithfulness! The Bible says, *"The eyes of the Lord run to and fro throughout the whole earth, to show himself strong in the behalf of them whose heart is perfect toward him"* (2 Chronicles 16:9). The word translated *perfect* there doesn't mean without a flaw. It simply means "faithful, loyal, dedicated and devoted."

God will pass over a million people to find that one who is loyal to Him. He scans the earth looking for people who will put Him first and let Him be God in their lives.

God wants to help us. He wants to move in our behalf. He wants to meet our every need and work miracles for us. If you were God, wouldn't you do that? Wouldn't you move in the lives of your children? The Bible says if you know how to give good gifts to your children, how much more the Father gives to His children (Luke 11:13).

Well, we're God's children. We've been born of His Spirit. We look just like God on the inside because He's our Father.

He has us in His heart. He cares about us. He loves each and every one of us as if each were the only child He had. God has a great and wonderful ability to have a family of many millions while treating every member as if they were the only one.

But God can't bless us as He wants if we won't let Him be God in our lives. He can't pour out His provision upon us if we keep clogging up our heavenly supply line by putting other things before Him. If He is to show Himself strong on our behalf, our hearts will have to be turned wholly toward Him.

Your Desire Follows Your Attention

Maybe today your heart isn't turned wholly toward God. Maybe you're facing the same situation I was facing back in 1977. You've grown busy and lost your appetite for the things of God. You know you ought to be praying more and spending more time in the Word, but you've lost your desire. You just don't want to do it.

If so, you can turn yourself around. You can rekindle your fire for the Lord by making the same kinds of changes I made. Before long, you'll find yourself addicted to God instead of the earthly pursuits that have been so consuming you.

How can I be so sure?

Because God showed me that your desire always follows your attention. Most people think it's the other way around. They think their attention follows their desire, but that's not the case.

One of the greatest practical examples of the fact that desire follows attention is the average golfer. In the springtime when the weather is nice and there is plenty of opportunity to play golf, most avid golfers become very absorbed in their sport. The more they play, the more they want to play.

They think about it, read about it, talk about it. They are constantly wanting to play golf!

But when winter comes, they put away their golf clubs. They stop talking about it and thinking about it. They don't mope around all winter because they can't be on the golf course. Why? Because they've turned their attention to other things, and their desire for golf has weakened.

I've seen that same principle at work in our conventions. People will come to a Believers' Convention, and when they arrive they will often be completely caught up in natural affairs. They'll be preoccupied, worrying and fussing about some business deal at the office or some problem they left at home.

But after just a day or two of attending the meetings and spending hours on end in the Word of God, they'll completely forget about that business deal and that problem. They'll be so absorbed in the Word that those things won't interest them at all.

It doesn't matter how disinterested you may have grown about the things of God.

If you will turn your attention toward Him, your heart will follow.

I know that from experience. I turned my attention to the Word of God, spent time listening to tapes, spent time in prayer until I became so addicted to the things of God that I lost interest in many of the other things that had so engaged me before. For example, I enjoy decorating homes and offices, and I used to spend a great deal of time at it. But as I became more involved in the things of God, I just didn't want to spend much time decorating. Now it's a chore to do that.

What's more, every time I thought about taking up some new project, starting a new hobby or buying something that would require me to spend my time maintaining it, I'd say to myself, *Can I afford this? Can I afford the time it will cost me?* Usually I decided I couldn't. I had come to value the things of God so much and have such great desire for them, I just didn't want to give my time to anything else unless it was absolutely necessary.

A Tithe of Your Time

My resolve to put my time in prayer and the Word first place every day was even further strengthened in 1982 by another prophecy by Kenneth E. Hagin. In that particular prophecy, the Spirit spoke of wading further out into the realm of the spirit, until it's so deep, you can't possibly touch the bottom. But, the Spirit warned, our flesh will hold us back from that. It's only by renewing our minds that we can move into the realm of the spirit. Brother Hagin went on to say by the Spirit of God that if we'd just give an hour or two out of every 24, our lives would be changed and empowered, all would be well, and we would be a mighty force for God.

That prophecy has influenced me and encouraged me tremendously throughout the years, and since I heard it, I have spent at least an hour or two alone with the Lord every day. When I began to do that, there were things in my life and family that I wanted to see changed. There were things in the lives of my children that needed to be improved.

When I heard the prophet say that if I'd spend an hour or two a day with the Lord, things would be well with me, I took God at His word. Today I can give testimony that word was true. It worked. At the writing of this article, everything in my life and the life of my family is good. Things are well with us. My children are healthy, blessed and serving the Lord.

There is no question about it. The time I've spent with God has changed my life. And I can say with certainty that if you'll spend an hour or two a day with Him, it will change your life, too.

How could it possibly be otherwise? How could you spend an hour or two daily with the highest authority and the most kind and loving Being in the universe without having it affect your life?

You may be facing problems today that seem to have no solutions. You may be caught in impossible circumstances. But I want you to know, God can change those things. If you'll give Him a way into your life by making living contact with Him every day, He'll give you a way out of those impossible circumstances. He'll help you solve those problems. He'll move on your behalf until you can say, "All is well with me!"

If you want a change, make a change. Commit yourself to do whatever it takes to maintain living contact with God and spend time with Him every day. Determine right now that by the strength and grace of God, if you have to get up earlier in the morning, you will do it. If you have to go to bed later at night, you will do it. If you have to change jobs, you will do it.

Decide that no matter what it takes, you will maintain your communion with God, and you will guard your heart above all, for out of it flow the issues of life.

Praying With Power

"The earnest (heartfelt, continued) prayer of a righteous man makes tremendous power available—dynamic in its working."
— JAMES 5:16, AMP

Terri Pearsons

The power of God. That, more than any other thing, is what we desperately need today. We need the power of God released in mighty ways to bring salvation, deliverance, healing and restoration into our lives, our families, our government and our world.

How do we tap into that power? It's no mystery, really. The Bible tells us very plainly in James 5:16: *"The earnest (heartfelt, continued) prayer of a righteous man makes tremendous power available—dynamic in its working"* (AMP).

But let's be honest. Every one of us has prayed prayers we felt weren't answered.

We've known people who prayed...and prayed...and prayed, but nothing happened. Those prayers didn't make tremendous, dynamic power available. Somehow they missed the mark.

We can't afford to miss the mark in prayer today. We must have dynamic power. It is essential in this hour. We must learn to stand up in the power of prayer and take dominion, bringing the will of God to pass on earth as it is in heaven.

In God's Image

"Dominion?" you ask. "I'm supposed to take dominion?"

Yes, you were destined and designed by God to be a ruler on this earth, not a victim of circumstance. You must clearly understand that you are to operate powerfully in prayer, because prayer is actually an act of dominion. Your job in prayer is to find the will of God concerning a particular situation, take hold of it in faith, and refuse to let go until this natural world submits to spiritual truth and God's will is carried out in that situation.

You might say that through prayer, you are to be the executor of God's will on the earth.

Does that surprise you? It shouldn't. It was God's plan from the very beginning. Genesis 1:26-28 says, *"And God said, Let us make man in our image, after our likeness: and let them have dominion...over all the earth...So God created man in his own image, in the image of God created he him; male and female created he them. And God blessed them, and God said unto them, Be fruitful, and multiply, and replenish the earth, and subdue it: and have dominion."*

Of course, God didn't intend to simply give man rulership of the earth and then just walk off and leave him with it. No, during those days in the Garden of Eden, He fellowshiped with man. He communed with him, walking with him in the cool of the day (Genesis 3:8). God designed mankind to be so in union with Him that together they would subdue this earth.

But something happened. Adam committed high treason. He disobeyed God and submitted himself to Satan and, therefore, to sin. The day he did that, the life and light of God was extinguished. Adam died spiritually and, as a result, he eventually died physically—and not just Adam but the whole race of man. As Romans 5:12 says, *"By one man sin entered into the world, and death by sin; and so death passed upon all men."*

A Reborn Race

It was a terrible tragedy, but even so, God would not go back on His Word. He had given mankind dominion, and it could never be reversed.

But God had a plan. He sent His own Son, Jesus, to the earth as a man. Born of the virgin Mary and of the incorruptible Word of God, this Son was born without the nature of sin in His spirit. He was born to be the last Adam (1 Corinthians 15:45). The first of a new race of men, a race who would be born of the Spirit in His image, a race that would once again reign in life as kings with the power and dominion of God.

Jesus lived His life on this earth as a perfect example of how this new race of man was to function. He didn't live as God, although He was divine. The Bible tells us that He let go of every divine privilege and power, *"made himself of no reputation, and took upon him the form of a servant, and was made in the likeness of men"* (Philippians 2:7).

Jesus was not sent to be an alien-type creature that we could look at and say, "Oh my, isn't He wonderful?" He came to be an example to us of how we could and should be. He came to demonstrate what God wanted to do through us.

If you'll read through the New Testament, one of the most striking things you'll see about Him is the fact that He walked in dominion wherever He went. Acts 10:38 says He *"went about doing good, and healing all that were oppressed of the devil."* There was nothing the devil could do to challenge Jesus successfully. Jesus was always in control. He cast out demons. He calmed the sea. He stopped the wind. He ended the fig tree's life. He healed the sick. He raised the dead. He multiplied food.

Those who witnessed His life and ministry *"were completely astonished at His teaching, for He was teaching as one who possessed authority, and not as the scribes...And they were all so amazed and almost terrified that they kept questioning and demanding one of another, saying, What is this? What new (fresh) teaching! With authority He gives orders even to the unclean spirits and they obey Him!"* (Mark 1:22, 27, AMP).

Even those who resisted Jesus and refused to acknowledge Him as sent from God recognized His dominion. *"And they kept saying to Him, By what (sort of) authority are You doing these things, or who gave You this authority to do them?"* (Mark 11:28, AMP).

Position + Relationship = Power

Because of His sinless life, Jesus walked in perfect dominion. God did whatever He asked, not because He was God's Son, but because He held the position of a righteous man. His prayers made much power available, dynamic in its working!

"But that was Jesus!" you say. "What does His prayer life have to do with mine?"

Everything—because the Bible says that through our believing on Him, we've been given the same position of righteousness with God that Jesus has. Ephesians 2:4-6 says it this way: *"But God, who is rich in mercy, for his great love wherewith he loved us, Even when we were dead in sins, hath quickened us together with Christ, (by grace ye are saved;) And hath raised us up together, and made us sit together in heavenly places in Christ Jesus."*

Just think, you're sitting in the seat of dominion with Jesus! You have the right to come boldly before God's throne of grace and obtain help and mercy in your time of need (Hebrews 4:16). You have a right to stand holy and blameless before God, not because of anything you did, but because you received the cleansing blood of Jesus.

So when the Bible talks about the right-eous man, it's talking about you!

If you've been around the Word of faith very long, you may be thinking, *Yes, I know I'm the righteousness of God in Christ Jesus. I know I have a position of right-standing with God, but my prayers are still lacking power!*

That's because position is not enough. You must also have the relationship. Jesus didn't rely purely on His position as a sinless man; He had communion with God. He fellowshiped with Him. You can see how vital that communion was in Mark 9.

There we see the disciples unable to cast the devil out of a demon-possessed boy. They knew they had the authority to do it because Jesus had given it to them, but for some reason they were unable to successfully exercise that authority. So after Jesus Himself had delivered the boy, *"His disciples asked Him privately, Why could not we drive it out? And He replied to them, This kind cannot be driven out by anything but prayer and fasting"* (verses 28-29, AMP).

Notice that Jesus didn't say, "You couldn't cast it out because you're not the sinless Son of God." He told them it was because of their lack of communion with God.

An Intimate Communion

The Bible doesn't reveal a great deal about Jesus' private communion with God through prayer. It does tell us that He spent 40 days in the wilderness before He began His ministry (Luke 4). It tells us that at times He got up a great while before day to pray (Mark 1:35). It tells us that He went into the hills to pray alone and that sometimes He prayed through the night (Luke 6:12).

How are we to know what went on during those prayer times? How can we be sure He was having communion with the Father? By studying the things He said, things such as:

> I assure you, most solemnly I tell you, the Son is able to do nothing from Himself—of His own accord; but He is able to do only what He sees the Father doing. For

91

whatever the Father does is what the Son does in the same way...My teaching is not My own, but His Who sent Me...He Who sent Me is true, and I tell the world [only] the things that I have heard from Him... I do nothing from Myself—of My own accord, or on My own authority—but I say [exactly] what My Father has taught Me (John 5:19, 7:16, 8:26, 28, AMP).

Jesus fellowshiped with the Father until He knew Him so well that He knew in every instance what the Father would say and do. He could answer and act on God's behalf because He knew God's heart and His ways.

We see that kind of thing happen in natural families all the time. A son might work with his father in business for so long that when the father retires, the son can run the business just as he did.

I know what that's like. I worked with my dad for so many years and listened to him preach so much that I knew what he'd say in almost any situation. If I had to edit one of his two-hour sermons to fit into a 45-minute television broadcast, I could do it without any problem. I knew exactly what points he'd want to leave in and what he'd want edited out.

Can you imagine knowing your Heavenly Father that well? It hardly seems possible, but it is!

That's what Jesus wanted us to see. That's why He left behind all the privileges of heaven. He wanted to show us the kind of communion man can have in relationship with God.

He wanted us to realize that through prayer we can develop our relationship with the Father. We can learn to walk with Him and commune with Him. We can tune in to Him and become one with Him just as Jesus was.

If we'll do that, Jesus said, *"Whatsoever ye shall ask the Father in my name, he will give it you"* (John 16:23). If that's not astonishing enough, He also said, *"He that believeth on me, the works that I do shall he do also; and greater works than these*

93

shall he do; because I go unto my Father"
(John 14:12).

Think for a moment. What works did
Jesus do? Those that He saw the Father do.
What words did He say? Those He heard
the Father say. So if we're going to do what
Jesus did, we too must see and hear from
the Father!

The Revealer Within You

"Well, I certainly don't know how I
could ever do that!"

You couldn't on your own. But, thank
God, Jesus didn't leave us on our own. He
sent us the Holy Spirit. In John 14 He
spoke of that Spirit, saying:

> I will ask the Father, and He
> will give you another Comforter
> (Counselor, Helper, Intercessor,
> Advocate, Strengthener and Standby)
> that He may remain with you
> forever, The Spirit of Truth, Whom
> the world cannot receive (welcome,
> take to its heart), because it does

not see Him, nor know and recognize Him. But you know and recognize Him, for He lives with you [constantly] and will be in you (verses 16-17, AMP).

Jesus considered the Holy Spirit so valuable that He said it was more profitable for us that He go away so the Spirit could come (John 16:7). That's because Jesus was limited to being with only a few people at a time, but the Holy Spirit is able to dwell with each and every one of us every second of every day.

Exactly what does the Holy Spirit do for us? Jesus tells us in John 16:

When He, the Spirit of Truth... comes, He will guide you into all the truth—the whole, full truth. For He will not speak His own message—on His own authority—but He will tell whatever He hears [from the Father, He will give the message that has been given to Him] and He will announce and declare to you the things that are to come...He will honor and glorify

Me, because He will take of (receive, draw upon) what is Mine and will reveal (declare, disclose, transmit) it to you. Everything that the Father has is Mine. That is what I meant when I said that He [the Spirit] will take the things that are Mine and will reveal (declare, disclose, transmit) them to you (verses 13-15, AMP).

How can you hear what the Father is saying? The Holy Spirit will tell you! How will you see what the Father is doing? The Holy Spirit will reveal Him to you! He'll enable you to commune with God, talk to Him and flow with Him just as Jesus did.

The Apostle John said it this way: *"But as for you, (the sacred appointment, the unction) the anointing which you received from [God], abides (permanently) in you; [so] then you have no need that any one should instruct you. But...His anointing teaches you concerning everything"* (1 John 2:27, AMP).

That verse doesn't mean we don't need teachers in the Body of Christ. It simply means you as an individual believer don't need anyone to tell you right from wrong. You don't need anyone to reveal God's will to you. You have this unction, this Holy One inside you, to lead you, talk to you and guide you. You have a knowing on the inside of you that comes from the Spirit of God.

This knowing enables you to first of all receive revelation from the written Word of God. Then as you look in that Word, the voice of the Spirit will begin to speak to you on the inside. The more time you spend in the Word and in prayer, the more familiar you'll become with that voice.

As the intimacy of that communion grows, you'll find yourself getting the kind of results in prayer you've always longed for. You'll not only step into the position of dominion, but also into an abiding relationship with God that opens the way for Him to give you all that you ask.

You'll discover firsthand the awesome truth recorded in James 5:16. *"The earnest... prayer of a righteous man makes tremendous power available—dynamic in its working"!* (AMP)

Pray Like Harvest Depends on It

"This is the confidence that we have in him, that, if we ask any thing according to his will, he heareth us: And if we know that he hear us, whatsoever we ask, we know that we have the petitions that we desired of him."
— 1 John 5:14-15

Kenneth Copeland

If there ever was a time we needed to pray, it is now.

It's a time for prayer because of the darkness the world is going through. Satan is killing people with diseases, drugs, depression and every other weapon he can get in his hands.

It's time to pray because this generation of believers is in a very, very special time in history. We are at the end of an age. The 6,000 years of man's lease (and Satan's lordship) on the earth are coming to a close.

The 1,000 years of Jesus' millennial reign are immediately ahead.

But before Jesus comes, God will fulfill every promise He has made during the 6,000 years of man's history on earth. The Body of the Anointed One is about to have its hands full of harvest.

The key to seeing the kind of results God wants His last-days generation to walk in is not just shooting some scattershot type of prayer and hoping something might happen. James wrote, *"Ye have not, because ye ask not. Ye ask, and receive not, because ye ask amiss, that ye may consume it upon your lusts"* (James 4:2-3). Success comes when we pray accurately according to the will of God.

Praying the Will of God

So many believers wring their hands and worry about whether or not they're praying according to God's will. Many of them have been taught a wrong view of God's sovereignty. They think that His ways are beyond finding out and that it is more spiritual to pray, "God, whatever Your will is in this situation, You just go ahead and do it."

Just think what kind of confusion that causes. Whatever results from that kind of praying is credited to God—good or bad! To really honor God's sovereignty, we must pray what He has already declared to be His will.

Praying the will of God is the only kind of praying that can consistently, confidently be expected to bring results. We weren't created to waste time standing around looking puzzled, especially in these days. We just need to grab our Bibles and find out what the will of God is. God's Word IS His will. He has made some very specific promises in it. And it's His will to fulfill every one of them.

Think about what you did when you prayed for salvation. You didn't pray, "God, I'm sick and tired of this life under Satan's control, and I want You to be my Lord and Savior. But I don't want to tell You what to do. Whatever Your will is—to set me free or to keep me in this miserable condition, to send me to heaven or to send me to hell—You just do it."

No. You prayed for God to save you just as His Word said He would. You prayed accurately according to His Word that He is *"not willing that any should perish"* (2 Peter 3:9). You prayed expecting results according to the promise that *"If thou shalt confess with thy mouth the Lord Jesus, and shalt believe in thine heart that God hath raised him from the dead, thou shalt be saved"* (Romans 10:9).

Maybe you wondered at first, *Did God hear me?* then later discovered that 1 John 5:14-15 says, *"If we ask any thing according to his will, he heareth us: And if we know that he hear us; whatsoever we ask, we know that we have the petitions that we desired of him."*

Find Out What the Word Says

These same principles work in any area of prayer. Do you need healing in your body? Don't pray what the doctor says or what your religious tradition has told you.

Pray, "By His stripes I am healed" (1 Peter 2:24). Do you have financial needs? Don't pray your problem. Pray what God has said He will do: "My God shall supply all my need according to His riches in glory by Christ Jesus" (Philippians 4:19).

God wants His will to be done on earth as it is done in heaven. Find the promise that applies to your situation, and pray the answer instead of the problem. Don't just pray what you remember the Word of God says. Read it! Even if you've read that promise a hundred times, read it again. Feed on what it says again and again. One day, you'll read a familiar verse and suddenly God will give you the greatest revelation you've ever had in your life. And it will be exactly what you needed to know to pray effectively about your current situation.

First John 5:14-15 says, *This is the confidence that we have in him, that, if we ask any thing according to his will, he heareth us: And if we know that he hear us, whatsoever we ask, we know that we have the petitions that we desired of him.*

When you pray God's Word knowing His will in advance, you are no longer praying just hoping to get results. You're not rattling off a bunch of religious-sounding words. You're praying expecting to get results. You're praying accurately because you are praying the very words God has given as His will to be done on earth.

So, before you pray, make the decision to get results. Then pray the Word, expecting God to move. That's the way we bring demonstrations of God's glory on earth while people are being increasingly tempted and terrorized by Satan's deception. That's the way we position ourselves to receive harvest that will come so quickly that the sower overtakes the reaper.

Jesus is the Alpha and Omega—the Beginning and the End—the First and Last. So let's start with His Word and finish with His Word. Give Jesus the first word in everything you do, and watch Him bring in a harvest like no previous generation has ever seen.

Fellowship: The Foundation of Powerful Prayer

Chapter 11

Lynne Hammond

"I know whom I have believed, and am persuaded that he is able to keep that which I have committed unto him against that day."
— 2 TIMOTHY 1:12

Judging strictly by appearances, it might seem that the Church of the Lord Jesus Christ is doing quite well in the area of prayer these days. Pick up almost any church bulletin in any city and you'll find listed midweek prayer meetings, prayer luncheons, prayer requests, perhaps even a printed prayer for the week.

Walk into any church service and you'll hear at least one prayer—probably two or three—before it's done. Listen in on the conversations of Christians and you'll hear them say, "I need you to pray for me, Brother." And, no doubt, you'll hear the same response every time, "Oh, yes. I will, I will."

One would think, with all this talk about prayer, the windows of heaven would be opened wide, spilling the blessings of God upon us. Jesus plainly promised that *"whatsoever ye shall ask in my name, that will I do, that the Father may be glorified in the Son"* (John 14:13). So we should be swimming in waves of revival, prosperity, healing and miracles of every sort. Our every conversation should be overflowing with joyful reports of answered prayer. The Church should be bursting forth with such earthshaking evidence of God's mighty delivering power, and sinners should be banging on our doors by the thousands, begging us to show them the way of salvation.

But clearly, that is not the case.

I do not mean to say we have seen no results from our praying. There have always been glimmers and even lightning strikes of the power and presence of God throughout the earth. There have been praying people and even praying congregations here and there who have moved mountains as they lifted their hearts to God—and every day their numbers are increasing. Yet even so, we must admit that in our day, the Church as a whole has not experienced what the Bible has promised would come to us through prayer.

Corporately, we have not seen buildings shake under the power of God as we unite in prayer as the Church did in Acts 4. Individually, we have not been able to speak with absolute certainty the words of the Apostle John: *"And this is the confidence that we have in him, that, if we ask any thing according to his will...we know that we have the petitions that we desired of him"* (1 John 5:14-15).

As a result, many Christians have allowed prayer to slip from their list of priorities. (One survey reported the average Christian invests less than two minutes a day at it.) Many others have struggled through the disappointments of unanswered prayer, trying to explain away their lack of results with theological arguments. "Well," they say, "perhaps it simply wasn't God's will this time."

But I believe every true Christian knows deep in his heart that despite what the theologians may say, our problem is not that God is saying a loving no to many of our requests. It's that our prayers too often lack the depth that heaven requires. They seem to come from the head, not the heart. Instead of being propelled from our spirit toward God with an earnestness and faith that cannot be denied, they often wobble from our uncertain lips and fall helplessly to the floor.

They have a form of godliness, but they deny the power thereof.

In times past, we were fooled by that form. We were like the shopper standing in the department store who sees the mannequin out of the corner of his eye and, thinking for a split second the mannequin is real, the shopper turns to speak to it.

But, praise God, we're not being fooled any more. We've looked that prayer mannequin square in the face and said, "You're not the real thing!"

We've turned our faces toward God and begun crying out as the disciples did two thousand years ago, "Lord, teach us to pray!"

And He is answering us. He is restoring to us not just the principles nor the mechanics, but the very spirit of prayer.

I Know Whom I Have Believed

It is that spirit we most desperately need. For although principles and formulas are valuable teaching tools, many times we have focused on them to the exclusion of God Himself. We have unwittingly grieved His tender Spirit by approaching Him almost as if He were a machine instead of a Person. We've followed step-by-step formulas as though by systematically pushing scriptural buttons and pulling spiritual levers, we could get Him to produce the results we desire.

Many of us have even recognized the truth—that it takes faith to receive from God. So we've studied the Bible, confessed particular verses over and over and memorized every key to spiritual success. Yet too often, instead of causing us to flourish in faith and prayer, our endeavors have left us dry and spiritless. Why is that? It is because we can't have real faith just by knowing principles. Real faith comes from knowing the Person behind the principles.

That's why the Apostle Paul in his great statement of faith wrote, *"I know whom I have believed, and am persuaded that he is able to keep that which I have committed unto him against that day"* (2 Timothy 1:12). Paul didn't say, "I know what I have believed." He didn't say, "I know the principles and steps I have believed." He said, "I know the Person of the Lord Jesus Christ."

You see, real praying comes from the heart hungry to know God. It comes when we cry out, as David did in Psalm 42: *"As the hart pants and longs for the water brooks, so I pant and long for You, O God. My inner self thirsts for God, for the living God... [Roaring] deep calls to [roaring] deep at the thunder of Your waterspouts; all Your breakers and Your rolling waves have gone over me"* (verses 1-2, 7, AMP).

When a person is hungry, the deepest part of his spirit begins to call out to God for something to fill that hunger. He might not even know what it is he is calling for, but God knows, and this cry touches the depths of His heart and causes Him to respond.

If we want true power in prayer, we must cultivate that kind of hunger. We must let the deep within us begin to call out to the deep in God. We must desire to know Jesus with such an intensity that every other desire pales beside it.

The fact is, however, that kind of desperate desire doesn't grow in the hearts of those whose relationships with God consist of simply going to church a couple times a week. It doesn't come to those who fellowship with God only at public gatherings of believers.

No, if we are to have true spiritual passion, we must develop a love affair with the Lord—and love affairs are never in public! We must seek out times of private, daily communion with Him, times of waiting before Him and worshiping Him. Instead of being content just to check in with Him now and then, we must learn to lift our hearts to Him continually, moment by moment.

You Can Pray Like Elijah!

Such constant and intimate fellowship is the key to vibrant and powerful prayer. For Jesus said, *"If you live in Me—abide vitally united to Me—and My words remain in you and continue to live in your hearts, ask whatever you will and it shall be done for you"* (John 15:7, AMP).

The word "ask" in that last verse has a far deeper meaning than most people realize. It implies you and God are so intertwined, your life and His life so closely joined together, that when you ask Him something, it's not really just you asking—it's Him asking, too.

That's the kind of asking that the Old Testament prophet Elijah did.

"Oh, Sister Hammond," you say, "I couldn't possibly pray with the power of Elijah."

Why not? The Bible says he was a human being just like we are (see James 5:16-18). He had all the same struggles and natural weaknesses we have. He is not set forth as an unusual fellow who lived off in the spiritual stratosphere somewhere. He is given to us as an inspiration and an example of earnest praying. Yet his prayers changed the course of nature. They changed people and nations. They projected God in full force to the world.

How was he able to do that?

Read 1 Kings 17 and you'll find out. There we see Elijah coming boldly before Ahab, the wicked king of Israel, announcing, *"As the Lord, the God of Israel lives, before Whom I stand, there shall not be dew or rain these years, but according to My word"* (verse 1, AMP).

Notice Elijah didn't just meander around. He didn't say, "Well, you know, I feel kind of impressed that it might be the Lord's will for rain not to fall around here for a while." No, he was firm and clear. He said, "Here's how it will be. Absolutely. Period. End of conversation." He reveals the reason for his confidence and power in the phrase *"the Lord, the God of Israel... before Whom I stand."*

That was the secret of Elijah's praying. He had stood in the power and presence of God. He didn't just make up those words he spoke to Ahab on his own. He received them from God Himself. In the times of fellowship, such as those he'd spent beside the brook Cherith alone with God, Elijah had come again and again before Him in prayer, and because he had stood in that place, he could speak and pray with world-shaking authority.

Make a Change

You and I have a far greater covenant than Elijah did. Through the precious blood of Jesus, God has opened for us a new and living Way so that we can come boldly before the throne of grace to obtain mercy and find grace to help in time of need (Hebrews 4:16). He has given us a freedom of access to Him the Old Testament saints never knew. He's made available to us all the resources and power of heaven.

But what have we done with those privileges? For the most part, we've done very little. We've been too busy making a living or watching television or perhaps even participating in church activities to take advantage of them. As a Church, we have pacified our spiritual hunger with the junk food the world has offered us, while we've let the dust collect on our Bibles and the cobwebs grow in our prayer closets.

Right now you may be thinking, *Yes, it's true. I have done that in the past, but I want to change it now. What can I do?*

Simply repent before God. Honestly acknowledge that you have desired other things more than Him. You cannot pretend to be hungry when you are not. But you can begin to call out to Him and say, "Lord, please forgive me and make me hungry for You."

You can, from this day on, say as David did, *"Your face, Lord, I will seek"* (Psalm 27:8, NIV). Set aside time to fellowship with God in prayer and in the Word every day, not out of a sense of religious duty, but because you want to whet your spiritual appetite and you know the fragrance of His presence as you meet Him daily in some quiet place will stir the hunger in your heart. It will awaken the craving that sleeps within every true child of God. It will remind you of how empty you are without Him and cause you to cry out from the depths of your soul, "Lord, I want to know You!"

In the natural course of this earth, wherever there's a vacuum, that vacuum causes the air to rush in and fill its emptiness. Thus, the wind blows there. The same is true in the spirit. If we'll empty ourselves of the distractions and desires of this world and crave Jesus alone, He will rush into our lives with the wind of the Holy Spirit. He will meet us with an intensity and an outpouring we have, until now, only read about in the pages of books.

We will know not just the form of prayer...but its power.

The Power
of Agreement

"If two of you agree on earth about anything that they may ask, it shall be done for them by My Father who is in heaven."
— MATTHEW 18:19, NAS

Kenneth Copeland

The prayer of agreement is one of the most powerful tools God has given us. It is a prayer that Jesus Himself guaranteed would bring results every time. *"If two of you agree on earth about anything that they may ask,"* He said, *"it shall be done for them by My Father who is in heaven"* (Matthew 18:19, NAS).

When you don't see the results He promised, I've found the problem usually lies in one of four areas.

1. Run a harmony check.

The word *agree* that Jesus uses in Matthew 18:19 can also be translated "to harmonize" or "to make a symphony." A symphony is composed of many instruments, which, when played together, seem to be a single voice.

If you've ever heard a symphony, you know that when the individual instruments are tuning up, each one playing separately from the other, it's not much to hear. But when the conductor raises his baton and all those instruments begin to harmonize, the sound they make is tremendously powerful.

The same thing is true in prayer. Believers agreeing together in the Holy Spirit are a powerful, unstoppable force. That's why Satan fights Christian families. That's why he doesn't want men and women unified in marriage. He wants us fighting and fussing all the time because he knows it will hinder our prayers (see 1 Peter 3:7).

Any time you fail to get results from the prayer of agreement, run a harmony check. Ask the Holy Spirit to show you if you're in strife with your wife (or anyone else). Then follow the instructions in Mark 11:25, where Jesus tells us, *"When ye stand praying, forgive, if ye have aught against any:*

that your Father also which is in heaven may forgive you."

It is not sufficient for you and your wife simply to agree on the particular issue you are praying about. You must also be in harmony in other areas as well. So make a harmony check!

2. Establish your heart on God's Word.

The prayer of agreement will only work if it is based on the Word of God. You and your wife might jump up one day and agree that you'll own a hundred oil wells by midnight, but you'll never see that prayer of agreement come to pass, because it's not founded on the Word of God.

So go to the Word first. Find the promise that covers the particular situation you're praying about. Then write it down and meditate on it until, as Psalm 112:7 says, your *"heart is fixed, trusting in the Lord."*

3. Fix your mind on the Word.

Second Corinthians 10:5 tells us to bring *"into captivity every thought to the obedience of Christ.*" You must do that if you're to see results from your prayers of agreement. Do what the Bible says and *"think on these things"* (Philippians 4:8). What things? Things from the Word of God!

Say to yourself, "I'll not think on anything contrary to this agreement." Then, when Satan tries to slip in negative thoughts and break down your faith, you'll have to tell him, "No, no, no, devil! I don't believe what you say. I believe what the Word says."

Then get out your Bible. Go back to the Word and soak your mind in it. Obey Proverbs 4 and "keep it before your eyes."

4. Act as if it's done.

This is where so many believers miss it. They pray the prayer of agreement, taking a faith stand together. Then as soon as they walk out of the prayer closet, they start wringing their hands and saying, "Oh my, I just don't know what we're going to do if this problem doesn't get solved!"

Don't make that mistake. Once you've settled the issue through the prayer of agreement, refuse to act as though that issue is a problem anymore. Instead, just start praising God. In every way you can, act as though all is well.

When people ask you about the matter, just answer them with faith. Say, "Glory to God, that issue is handled. My wife and I have agreed in prayer. God is honoring our agreement. And as far as we're concerned, that problem is behind us."

The prayer of agreement is a powerful tool. So don't be discouraged by your past experience. Just make the necessary adjustments, and keep on in agreement. Run a harmony check. Establish your heart on the Word. Fix your mind on the Word. Act as if it's done. And anything you ask shall be done for you by your Father in heaven.

A Blaze of Praise: The Secret of Supernatural Combustion

Chapter 13

Gloria
Copeland

"Let the saints be joyful in glory...Let the high praises of God be in their mouth, and a twoedged sword in their hand."
— PSALM 149:5-6

Something peculiar is happening to believers these days. They're beginning to rejoice.

If you've been in many meetings where the Holy Spirit has moved, you know what I mean. God is pouring out a spirit of joy so strong it causes people to laugh for hours. Some of them literally end up on the floor doubled over laughing with the joy of the Lord.

Recently, during the Southwest Believers' Convention, that joy swept through the convention center, affecting literally thousands of people. It so filled Ken that he could hardly minister. The next morning, however, he could not only stand and preach, he felt stronger than he'd felt in 10 years.

That's supernatural...but it's not surprising, because the Bible says, *"The joy of the Lord is your strength"* (Nehemiah 8:10).

I have to tell you, though, when God's people start to praise Him and rejoice with that kind of abandon—it makes some Christians nervous. As a result, many of them are folding their arms, sitting back, saying, "I'm not going to be caught acting like that"...and as a result, they're missing out on a powerful move of God.

I don't want that to happen to you. I don't want you to hold back when the Spirit of God is moving. I want you to be able to step by faith into His flow and receive the rich blessings He's pouring out in these last days.

I'm confident that's what you want, too. So let me share with you a few things I've learned about rejoicing from the Word of God.

Tell "Dignity" Goodbye

Some years ago, when I first began to catch sight of the supernatural power of joy, I did a study on it. During that study, I discovered that one of the biblical words for *joy* is translated "to shine." Another word means "to leap." Another means "to delight." But in every case, joy is more than an attitude; it is an action.

As I studied, I also found out that joyful praise gives God pleasure. Psalm 149 says: *"Praise ye the Lord. Sing unto the Lord a new song, and his praise in the congregation of saints. Let Israel rejoice in him that made him: let the children of Zion be joyful in their King. Let them praise his name in the dance: let them sing praises unto him with the timbrel and harp. For the Lord taketh pleasure in his people"* (verses 1-4).

It doesn't offend God when we boisterously praise Him. He likes it. It gives Him pleasure to see us shine and leap and express our delight in Him.

"Let the saints be joyful in glory...Let the high praises of God be in their mouth, and a twoedged sword in their hand" (verses 5-6).

I know that by natural standards, that kind of exuberant praise doesn't look very dignified. But as believers, we need to get past the point where we care about that. We need to focus instead on pleasing God. We should have such a desire to please Him that we don't care how we look to other people.

"But, Gloria, that's easy for you to say. You're comfortable with expressing yourself to God in praise."

I haven't always been. I was so conservative when I first began to walk with God that it took me a long time to even begin to lift my hands in praise. But I broke through that "dignity," and so can you.

Of course, there are always some believers who try to please God and look good at the same time by "praising God quietly in their hearts." Although there's a time for quiet worship, the Bible says joy isn't always quiet. In fact, joy shouts.

"But let all those that put their trust in thee rejoice: let them ever shout for joy, because thou defendest them" (Psalm 5:11).

You may not know this, but when you get to heaven, it's not going to be quiet. The throne room of God is a noisy place. Isaiah 6 tells us: *"In the year that king Uzziah died I saw also the Lord sitting upon a throne, high and lifted up, and his train filled the temple. Above it stood the seraphims...And one cried unto another, and said, Holy, holy, holy, is the Lord of hosts: the whole earth is full of his glory. And the posts of the door moved at the voice of him that cried, and the house was filled with smoke"* (verses 1-4).

The throne room is a loud place that's filled with the glory of God. Living ones are crying *"Holy, holy, holy"* until the very door posts shake!

I'm telling you, God is not all laid back as some people think. He is not getting old. He isn't even slowing down. His very presence causes people to get so excited they shout.

Do you ever go to a football game and cheer and shout? Is that normal? Certainly! You'd look pretty strange sitting silently on the bench trying to look dignified.

Well, I think it's normal when we get excited worshiping God. In the throne room they think it's normal to cry, "Holy, holy, holy is the Lord God Almighty. The whole earth is full of His glory!"

That's what's normal up there. So if we're going to pray, *"Thy kingdom come, Thy will be done on earth as it is in heaven,"* then we need to learn to act down here as they act up there. We need to learn a holy shout!

Is Jesus Nervous?

Now let's see what Jesus says about praising God. After all, He's the Head of the Church. If He gets nervous when people start praising loudly, then we'd better slow down. (But I've already looked this up, and I know He doesn't.) I'll tell you who did get nervous, though—the Pharisees.

The Gospel of Luke tells us about a time when *"the whole multitude of the disciples began to rejoice and praise God with a loud voice for all the mighty works that they had seen...And some of the Pharisees from among the multitude said unto him, Master, rebuke thy disciples"* (Luke 19:37-39).

The Pharisees didn't like that kind of praise. But that's not surprising. The religious folks didn't like anything Jesus did, because nothing He did fit their traditions. And, since they'd lost the power of God in their lives, tradition was all they had!

Make a note of this: When you lose contact with the power of God, you lose your excitement about worship. You start adopting traditions and rituals—and if anyone violates those, it offends you.

That's what happened to the Pharisees. How do you think Jesus responded? Do you think He restrained His disciples so they wouldn't offend anyone? No. He said, *"I tell you that, if these should hold their peace, the stones would immediately cry out"* (Luke 19:40).

Jesus never tried to please the Pharisees. He only pleased God. He just told them, "If my disciples don't praise Me, the rocks will do it!" That's what Jesus thinks about praise. He's in favor of it—no matter how badly it bothers some folks.

Your Greatest Desire

When we become like Jesus and desire God so intensely that we're willing to cast aside our desire to please men and praise Him without reserve, we'll truly see the glory of God.

Why? Because God manifests Himself where He's wanted. He shows up where hearts are hungry. He's not going to reveal Himself to a great degree among people whose hearts are partially turned to Him and partially turned toward something else.

God told Moses, *"As truly as I live, all the earth shall be filled with the glory of the Lord"* (Numbers 14:21). That's what He wants. He's wanted it for a very long time. But He has to have a people who will allow Him to be their God—with nothing else before Him. They have to want Him and His presence more than they want to be respected in their neighborhood. They have to want Him more than anything else life has to offer.

Today He is finding people who are willing to do that. People who literally praise God with all their heart.

If you are one of those people, you've probably already found out that some people don't like it. The glory of God offends them, and they don't want to be around you.

Not surprisingly, very often it is the religious people who will criticize you most harshly. After Jesus healed the blind man, the religious leaders told him, "Don't give that Jesus any credit—He's a sinner" (John 9:24, my paraphrase).

The sick, hungry people of the world won't say things like that. They're not like the people who have been "religionized." They want help and they don't care where they get it.

They have the same attitude as the man who was born blind. He said to the Pharisees, *"Whether he (Jesus) be a sinner or no, I know not: one thing I know, that whereas I was blind, now I see"* (verse 25).

Now That's Power!

If you're not sure you have the strength to face the criticism of the religious people, I have good news for you. You can get that strength by rejoicing, because the Bible says, *"The joy of the Lord is your strength"* (Nehemiah 8:10).

Joy and praise together release strength on the inside of you and power on the outside. Psalm 9:1-3 says it this way: *"I will praise thee, O Lord, with my whole heart; I will show forth all thy marvellous works. I will be glad and rejoice in thee: I will sing praise to thy name, O thou most High. When mine enemies are turned back, they shall fall and perish at thy presence."*

God inhabits our praises (Psalm 22:3). And when His presence begins to come into our midst, our enemies fall back. They can't stand the presence of God. *"Let God arise, let his enemies be scattered: let them also that hate him flee before him. As smoke is driven away, so drive them away: as wax melteth before the fire, so let the wicked perish at the presence of God. But let the righteous be glad; let them rejoice before God: yea, let them exceedingly rejoice"* (Psalm 68:1-3).

Now that's power! When God's people rise up in praise and worship and celebrate the victories of God, His enemies are scattered.

No wonder Satan has tried so hard to get God's people to sit still. No wonder he has bound us up with traditions that taught us to sit back in dignified silence. (The word *dignity* means "to be self-possessed.") For most of us, our traditions have taught us not to do the very things the Bible says we are to do when we worship and praise.

Burn, Brother, Burn!

But tradition's day is over. I'm telling you, when the Spirit begins to move, inhibition has to flee. The Bible says, *"And they...shall be like a mighty man, and their heart shall rejoice as through wine"* (Zechariah 10:7).

You know what happens when people drink wine—they lose their inhibitions! That's what happened to the disciples on the Day of Pentecost. They had been hiding out only days before, but when the Holy Ghost came upon them, suddenly they were out on the streets acting so wild everyone thought they'd been drinking.

Listen, what God considers "dignified" and what you consider dignified are two different things. God wants you free. He doesn't want you bound up with traditions or fear of what other people might think.

He wants you free to laugh. He wants you free to leap and praise and sing. He wants you free to rejoice. He wants you so free that other people won't understand it—they'll just want it!

Never underestimate the drawing power of joy. It's like a blazing fire that captures the attention of people in darkness. In fact, in a dream I had many years ago, God called it "spontaneous combustion."

I didn't even know what the term meant until the next day. When I looked it up in a dictionary, here's what I found: *Spontaneous combustion*—"the process of catching fire and burning as a result of heat generated by an internal chemical reaction."

That's it! Joy—the process of catching fire and burning as a result of heat which comes from the Holy Ghost.

It's time to rejoice, to rise up out of our exhaustion and implement the power of praise. When you do, you'll enter a domain of power, freedom and the joy of the Lord. A domain that's alive and shining with the presence of God.

So throw off those old inhibitions. Take God at His Word. Leap. Shout. Sing. Let yourself catch fire in the Spirit and never stop burning.

Prayer for Salvation and Baptism in the Holy Spirit

Heavenly Father, I come to You in the Name of Jesus. Your Word says, *"Whosoever shall call on the name of the Lord shall be saved"* (Acts 2:21). I am calling on You. I pray and ask Jesus to come into my heart and be Lord over my life according to Romans 10:9-10. *"If thou shalt confess with thy mouth the Lord Jesus, and shalt believe in thine heart that God hath raised him from the dead, thou shalt be saved. For with the heart man believeth unto righteousness; and with the mouth confession is made unto salvation."* I do that now. I confess that Jesus is Lord, and I believe in my heart that God raised Him from the dead.

I am now reborn! I am a Christian—a child of Almighty God! I am saved! You also said in Your Word, *"If ye then, being evil, know how to give good gifts unto your children: HOW MUCH MORE shall your heavenly Father give the Holy Spirit to them that ask him?"* (Luke 11:13). I'm also asking You to fill me with the Holy Spirit. Holy Spirit, rise up within me as I praise God. I fully expect to speak with other tongues as You give me the utterance (Acts 2:4).

Begin to praise God for filling you with the Holy Spirit. Speak those words and syllables you receive—not in your own language, but the language given to you by the Holy Spirit. You have to use your own voice. God will not force you to speak. Worship and praise Him in your heavenly language—in other tongues.

Continue with the blessing God has given you and pray in tongues each day.

You are a born-again, Spirit-filled believer. You'll never be the same!

Find a good Word of God preaching church, and become a part of a church family who will love and care for you as you love and care for them.

We need to be hooked up to each other. It increases our strength in God. It's God's plan for us.

Books Available
From
Kenneth Copeland Ministries

by Kenneth Copeland
* A Ceremony of Marriage
  A Matter of Choice
  Covenant of Blood
  Faith and Patience—The Power Twins
* Freedom From Fear
  Giving and Receiving
  Honor—Walking in Honesty, Truth and Integrity
  How to Conquer Strife
  How to Discipline Your Flesh
  How to Receive Communion
  Living at the End of Time—
       A Time of Supernatural Increase
  Love Never Fails
  Managing God's Mutual Funds
* Now Are We in Christ Jesus
* Our Covenant With God
* Prayer—Your Foundation for Success
* Prosperity: The Choice Is Yours
  Rumors of War
* Sensitivity of Heart
* Six Steps to Excellence in Ministry
  Sorrow Not! Winning Over Grief and Sorrow
* The Decision Is Yours
* The Force of Faith
* The Force of Righteousness
  The Image of God in You
  The Laws of Prosperity
* The Mercy of God
  The Miraculous Realm of God's Love
  The Outpouring of the Spirit—The Result of Prayer
* The Power of the Tongue
  The Power to Be Forever Free
  The Troublemaker
* The Winning Attitude

Turn Your Hurts Into Harvests
* Welcome to the Family
* You Are Healed!
Your Right-Standing With God

by Gloria Copeland
* And Jesus Healed Them All
Are You Ready?
Build Your Financial Foundation
Build Yourself an Ark
Fight On!
God's Prescription for Divine Health
God's Success Formula
God's Will for You
God's Will for Your Healing
God's Will Is Prosperity
* God's Will Is the Holy Spirit
* Harvest of Health
Hidden Treasures
Living Contact
Living in Heaven's Blessings Now
* Love—The Secret to Your Success
No Deposit—No Return
Pleasing the Father
Pressing In—It's Worth It All
Shine On!
The Power to Live a New Life
The Unbeatable Spirit of Faith
This Same Jesus
* Walk in the Spirit
Walk With God
Well Worth the Wait

Books Co-Authored by Kenneth and Gloria Copeland
Family Promises
Healing Promises
Prosperity Promises

* From Faith to Faith—A Daily Guide to Victory
From Faith to Faith—A Perpetual Calendar

One Word From God Series
- One Word From God Can Change Your Destiny
- One Word From God Can Change Your Family
- One Word From God Can Change Your Finances
- One Word From God Can Change Your Health

Over the Edge—A Youth Devotional
Over the Edge Xtreme Planner for Students—
    Designed for the School Year

Pursuit of His Presence—A Daily Devotional
Pursuit of His Presence—A Perpetual Calendar

Other Books Published by KCP
The First 30 Years—A Journey of Faith
    The story of the lives of
        Kenneth and Gloria Copeland.
Real People. Real Needs. Real Victories.
    A book of testimonies to encourage your faith.

John G. Lake—His Life, His Sermons,
    His Boldness of Faith
The Holiest of All by Andrew Murray
The New Testament in Modern Speech by
    Richard Francis Weymouth

Products Designed for Today's Children and Youth
Baby Praise Board Book
Noah's Ark Coloring Book
The *Shout!* Super-Activity Book

Commander Kellie and the Superkid Adventure Novels
#1 The Mysterious Presence
#2 The Quest for the Second Half
#3 Escape From Jungle Island
#4 In Pursuit of the Enemy

SWORD Adventure Book

* Available in Spanish

WE'RE HERE FOR YOU!

Join Kenneth and Gloria Copeland and the *Believer's Voice of Victory* broadcast Monday through Friday and every Sunday. Learn how faith in God's Word can take your life from ordinary to extraordinary.

It's some of the most in-depth teaching you'll ever hear on subjects like faith and healing, deliverance and prosperity, protection and hope. And it's all designed to get you where you want to be—*on top!* The teachings are by some of today's best-known ministers, including Kenneth and Gloria Copeland, Jerry Savelle, Charles Capps, Creflo A. Dollar Jr., Kellie Copeland and Edwin Louis Cole.

Whether it's before breakfast, during lunch or after a long day at the office, plan to make *Believer's Voice of Victory* a daily part of your prayer life. See for yourself how one word from God can change your life forever.

You can catch the *Believer's Voice of Victory* broadcast on the following cable and satellite channels:

Sunday
9-9:30 p.m. ET
Cable*/G5,
Channel 3—TBN

Monday through Friday
7-7:30 p.m. ET
Cable*/G1,
Channel 17—INSP

Monday through Friday
6-6:30 a.m. ET
Cable*/G5,
Channel 7—WGN

Monday through Friday
11-11:30 a.m. ET
Cable*/G5,
Channel 3—TBN

Monday through Friday
6:30-7 a.m. ET
Cable*/G5,
Channel 20—BET

Monday through Friday
10:30-11 a.m. CT
Cable*/Spacenet 3,
Transponder 13 - KMPX

*Check your local listings for more times and stations in your area.

WE'RE HERE FOR YOU!

Believer's Voice of Victory Television Broadcast

Join Kenneth and Gloria Copeland and the *Believer's Voice of Victory* broadcasts Monday through Friday and on Sunday each week, and learn how faith in God's Word can take your life from ordinary to extraordinary. This is some of the best teaching you'll ever hear, designed to get you where you want to be— *on top!*

You can catch the *Believer's Voice of Victory* broadcast on your local, cable or satellite channels.

* Check your local listings for
times and stations in your area.

Believer's Voice of Victory Magazine

Enjoy inspired teaching and encouragement from Kenneth and Gloria Copeland each month in the *Believer's Voice of Victory* magazine. Also included are real-life testimonies of God's miraculous power and divine intervention into the lives of people just like you!

It's more than just a magazine—it's a ministry.

Shout! ...The dynamic magazine just for kids!

Shout! The Voice of Victory for Kids is a Bible-charged, action-packed, bimonthly magazine available FREE to kids everywhere! Featuring *Wichita Slim* and *Commander Kellie and the Superkids*, *Shout!* is filled with colorful adventure comics, challenging games and puzzles, exciting short stories, solve-it-yourself mysteries and much more!!

Stand up, sign up and get ready to *Shout!*

World Offices
of Kenneth Copeland Ministries

For more information about KCM and a free
catalog, please write the office nearest you:

Kenneth Copeland Ministries
Fort Worth, TX 76192-0001

Kenneth Copeland
Locked Bag 2600
Mansfield Delivery Centre
QUEENSLAND 4122
AUSTRALIA

Kenneth Copeland
Post Office Box 15
BATH
BA1 1GD
ENGLAND U.K.

Kenneth Copeland
Private Bag X 909
FONTAINEBLEAU
2032
REPUBLIC OF SOUTH AFRICA

Kenneth Copeland
Post Office Box 378
Surrey
BRITISH COLUMBIA
V3T 5B6
CANADA

UKRAINE
L'VIV 290000
Post Office Box 84
Kenneth Copeland Ministries
L'VIV 290000
UKRAINE

The Harrison House Vision

Proclaiming the truth and the power
Of the Gospel of Jesus Christ
With excellence;

Challenging Christians to
Live victoriously,
Grow spiritually,
Know God intimately.